D1306458

MIX & MATCH JOKES

Library of Congress Catalog-in-Publication Data
Woodworth, Viki
Mix and match jokes / Written and illustrated by Viki Woodworth.
p. cm.
Summary: A collection of riddles about what happens
when you cross hummingbirds and bells, bees and guns,
skeletons and fairy godmothers, and other such unlikely combinations.
ISBN 1-56766-063-0
1. Wit and humor, Juvenile 2. Riddles, Juvenile.
[1. Riddles 2. Jokes.]
I. Title.
PN6163.W69 1994   92-38580
818.5402–dc20   CIP/AC

MIX & MATCH JOKES

Compiled and Illustrated by
Viki Woodworth

THE CHILD'S WORLD

What do you get if you cross a fig with a gnu?

A fig gnuton.

Jane: What do you get when you cross a virus with a comic?

Eric: Sick jokes.

What do you get when you cross a telephone and a shirt?

Ring around the collar.

Eric: What do you get when you cross a bee with a gun?

Jane: A bee-bee gun.

What do you get when you cross a pen with a banana?

A ball-point banana.

What do you get when you cross a snake and a necktie?
A boa-tie.

What do you get when you cross a pile of dirt with a frog?

A sod-hopper.

Alice: What do you get when you cross a country bumpkin with a frog?

A clod-hopper.

What do you get if you cross a funny person with a motorcycle?

A Yama-haha.

What do you get if you cross a newspaper with a sleeping person?

A snooze paper.

What do you get when you cross a pair of glasses with a potato?

A spectator.

What do you get when you cross a restaurant with a chicken?

A roosterant.

What do you get when you cross a hippo with a dictionary?

Big words.

Ann: What do you get when you cross a rhino and a pumpkin?

Heidie: Squash.

What do you get when you cross a pine tree with a pig?

A porky-pine.

Heidie: What do you get when you cross a duck with a casserole dish?

Ann: Quackeroni and cheese.

What do you get when you cross a criminal with a rooster?

A Crook-a-doodle-doo.

What do you get when you cross an elephant with a poker game?
A big deal.

What do you get when you cross a strongman with a tailor?
Popeye the tailorman.

Molly: What do you get when you cross a wood-cutter with a sleepy person?
Peter: A slumberjack.

What do you get when you cross a taxi with grass seed?
Cab grass.

Peter: What do you get when you cross a locomotive with bubble gum?
Molly: A chew-chew train.

What do you get when you cross a tuba with a daddy?
An Ooom-papa.

What do you get when you cross a pig with a tiger?
Striped sausages.

What do you get when you cross a thief with a candy bar?

Hot chocolate.

What do you get when you cross a camel with a cot?

A lumpy bed.

Emily: What do you get when you cross a sheep with a storm?

James: A wet blanket.

What do you get when you cross two bananas with shoes?

A pair of slippers.

What do you get when you cross a snowman with a bowl of cereal?

Frosty Flakes.

What do you get when you cross a storm with a deer?
Raindeer.

What do you get when you cross a pig with a tub?

Hogwash.

Nora: What do you get when you cross a teddy bear with a ghost?

Charlotte: Winnie-The-Boo.

What do you get when you cross soda pop with a frog?

Croaka Cola.

Charlotte: What do you get when you cross a dog with a bouquet?

Nora: Collie-flowers.

What do you get when you cross a tiger and a parrot?

I'm not sure, but when it talks, you better listen!

What do you get if you cross a lawn mower with a cow?
A lawn moo-er.

What do you get when you cross a toad with a dog?

A croaker spaniel.

Michael: What do you get when you cross a dog with a sad person?

Chris: A melan-collie.

What do you get when you cross a cat and an Old West Sheriff?

A posse cat.

Chris: What do you get when you cross a cat with a big hill?

Michael: A meowntain.

What do you get when you cross mice with ice?

Micecicles.

What do you get if you cross a dinosaur with a jar of peanut butter?

A jar of peanut butter with big feet.

What do you get when you cross a giraffe and a flower?

A giraff-odil.

Rebecca: What do you get when you cross a monkey with a flower?

Anna: Chimpansies.

What do you get when you cross a chimp and a tool?

A monkey wrench.

Anna: What do you get when you cross hot chocolate with a duck?

Rebecca: Nestle's Quack?

What do you get when you cross a phony doctor with a duck?

A quack quacker.

What do you get if you cross a shark with hard candy?
A jaw breaker.

19

What do you get when you cross a diplomat with a dog?

A diplo-mutt.

Marit: What do you get when you cross a cow with a school official?

Peggy: A princi-bull.

What do you get when you cross a cat with a tired person?

A cat nap.

What do you get when you cross a baby cat with a tired person?

Marit: A sitten' kitten.

What do you get when you cross a baby cat with a ball of yarn?

A mitten.

What do you get if you cross a pair of shoes with bread?
Loafers.

What do you get when you cross an acrobat with a bee?

A tumble-bee.

Patrick: What do you get when you cross a modest person with a bee?

Daniel: A humble-bee.

What do you get when you cross a bee with ground meat?

A humburger.

What do you get when you cross a rabbit with a bee?

A bunny-bee.

What do you get when you cross a cow with a person who borrows a lot?

A moo-cher.

What do you get when you cross a cow with a criminal?
A cud thug.